Closed Conversations

JOHN PAUL

First published 2020 by John Paul
PO Box 673, Mulgrave Victoria 3170 Australia.

Copyright © John Paul, 2020
The moral rights of the author have been asserted

ISBN (hardback): 978-0-6488533-4-3
ISBN (paperback): 978-0-6489252-1-7

This book is copyright. Except for private study, research, criticism or reviews, as permitted under the *Australian Copyright Act 1968*, no part of this book may be reproduced, stored in a retrieval system, or transmitted in any form or by any means without prior written permission. Enquiries should be made to the author.

Many thanks to Brook Emery for his mentorship in the early works and to Luke Harris for his guidance and talents.

Cover and Design by Working Type Studio
Man and boy on bench sketch by Pawel.
Other designs by Working Type Studio.
Moon footprint courtesy of the
National Aeronautical and Space Administration

Silverbird Publishing Pty Ltd
PO Box 72, Eltham Victoria 3095 Australia

To Gummo, Peachcobbler and Strudel

With Love

Epigraph

This has been written not for the many
but for the crowd of one as this is aplenty.[1]

But if these muses find you dear reader
the atheist agnostic or believer

either in sync or with disdain
know that this is a contemplative refrain.

With a heart laid bare in full view of your glare
one will proceed without care.

---

1 With apologies to Epicurus.

Table of Contents

Epigraph iv
Table of Contents v
Preface 1
A New Rise 3
With Gratitude and Apologies 4
Just Be Insitu 6
Primordial Soup 8
Decibels and Hues 9
The Pursuit of Knowledge 10
Without Words 12
I for U 14
The Deft Touch 15
The Relativity of Love and Pain 16
Unmediated 17
Wishful Promises 18
Thieves All in All 19
Minority 20
The Counsellor's Lament 21
Dyslexia 22
The Shape of Reality 24
Your Promised Land 26
The Art of Wisdom 28
The Imaginary Card 29
Be Without 30

Virtue Plunges on Affluenzavirus 32
Contentment and Happiness 34
Perspective 35
Elders 37
The Elegant Solution 38
Vision Impaired 39
Belief Systems 40
Knowledge and Belief 41
The Orphan 42
Irrelevant 43
The Rake of Hope and Fear 44
Family 45
Cunabula de Natura 46
The Cycle of Life 47
Place of Last Resort 48
Names   Perceptions and Destiny 49
In Perpetuity 50
Where Capable Meets Incapable 51
History 52
Squandering Longevity 53
Undressing Room of Solitude 54
In the Now 55
Hermitage 56
Gummo 57
The Betrayal 58
Edinburgh Castle 59
Clusters of Affinity 60
Our Wish 61

The Ageing Season	64
Missing You Already	66
Nothing to Fear Nothing Unjust	68
All That Remains	70
Epilogue	71
The Realist's Interprenary	73

Preface

Implacable eddies of discontent
belching from fissures rooted in lament
would be insignificant if to hold what is
and resist that devoid of nature's premise.

Infancy is imbued with this appreciation
yet as if by Darwinian declaration
the clarity of youthful resolution
is dimmed like cataracts seared from life's irradiation.

Corroding the soul's protective sheath
venting essence in an atmosphere of disbelief
dislodging rhythm and equilibrium
like a knave spring within natura's pendulum.

Experience wanders and wonders with disillusion
failingly protecting the inner   drenched in confusion
retreating from the wanton pricks of the exoteric
caulking the leaks of diminution at a rate frenetic.

Descry the youth parked on the mantel shelf
alone   calmly awaiting the elder self
a smile   an embrace   a knowing manner
closed conversations awash with candour.

A New Rise

Shut the door on the past
turn the key   do it fast
pull the chord draw the curtain
be empowered   firm and certain

Do you not see old man
we arrived at our destination   contentment in hand
as of now from the view of the herd
we are as desired   small   no longer heard

But within   now that is something else again
essence intact   resilience retained
an obscured citadel amongst men
employed with effect every now and then

Sidestep the pain of time and resistance
these are far less grievous than engagement or insistence
within hours there is the sunrise
venture outside   look around   step forward   thrive

With Gratitude and Apologies

Thank you for the bestowal of life
at a time and place remote from strife.

Thank you for the roof   the accoutrements and sustenance
marshalled from meagre resource   provided in abundance.

Thank you for planting me peripherally in early years
where self-sovereignty flowered   irrigated by tears.

Thank you for quarantining me from the past
and selecting a means that failed at the last.

Thank you for acceding to my curiosity
despite its draining of resource and perceived futility.

Thank you for the gift of resilience and fortitude
standing at the ready when occasion brews.

                    I am sorry for arriving at an adverse time
              unwittingly displacing your truncated prime.

                    I am sorry that what you saw
              was not who I am but an 'educated bore'.

I am sorry that each was not bathed
in amniotic affection so sorely craved.

I am sorry for all my highs and lows
consigned to ambivalence   forever disposed.

I am sorry for the stream of failures
that combusted hopes to smouldering embers.

I am sorry for all the memories excised by pain
belligerently discarded   posthumously inane.

I am sorry that at the age of eight
I chased weeping as you drove from the gate.

I am sorry that my loves were not embraced
in the manner that they graced.

I am sorry that innate ethics and equity
were systemically violated with impunity.

I am sorry that love so dearly sought
remained unrequited deep within my thought.

Just Be Insitu

It is not quiet condemnation that prohibits association
for there is much that appeals in the embrace of congregation
community has its grace   for most there is no other place
but you my boy will struggle with the human race.

All that is life ebbs and flows
like Mary Poppins[2]   presence comes and goes
for some events   in fleeting times
you will belong   seemingly entwined.

But as vigorously as these arise they evaporate
leaving you again in a detached state
then with fervour that leaves others aghast
you blissfully abscond   discarding the past.

The eyes bear faithful witness to that as is
whether in plain view or in a crevice
it is voice and scribe that should be jeered
concealing all to be believed.

---

2   Apologies to P.L. Travers.

With haste   dislodge the tartar of judgment
that dissolves the inner with intent
seek not above for they are not
nor from below for they cannot.

For all you are and will be
proffers no promise to belong or even agree
know that your vision is true   hold its clarity as virtue
you are okay   just be insitu.

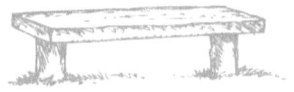

Primordial Soup

An endless primordial soup of mystical potions
sourced from leptons   quarks   fermions and bosons
ephemeral transpirations abiding instruction
harmonised in the cosmic crucible   ushering succession.

None with ethnicity   gender or colour
none with   class   belief or power
none from regions or with accents
much less the vast array of descendants.

Each timeless   omnipresent   an enigma
unbridled from thought   free from stigma
circuitous between minimum and maximum
companions all in a zero-sum sanctum.

Decibels and Hues

In the Universe Theatre at a location near you
reality's uncredited movie is perennially on view.
An endless panorama of decibels and hues
inlaying the spirit with wonder and virtue.

Cosmic images on an infinite screen
a drama of unfathomable beauty and violence extreme.
Spoken in dialogue unbeknown
inviting interpretation with illiterate undertone.

A cinematic experience of innumerable takes
a galaxy of stars illuminating light   sounding quakes.
A plot without pretext or message within
only the reverent chronicle of the unity therein.

The Pursuit of Knowledge

Part 1 – *The Expedition*

Conceived from a spark of curiosity
igniting frenetic rounds of trial and conjecture
a pugilistic contest of incremental convergence
between evidence in one corner and theorem in the other.

Contestants encircle on a canvas of reality's guiles
awash in the perspiration of unbridled intensity
deriding disquisition of a clandestine nature
adjudicated by the tally of uncertainty.

Part 2 – *The Opposition*

The magma of ignorance lies deep within contemplation
percolating with alacrity throughout the congregation
expunged by the omnipresence of dogma and smear
cooled   then solidified by a climate of fear.

Compiled as arrays of syllables and graphics
streamed diuretically through digital prosthetics
relentlessly anaesthetising the elegance of reality
asphyxiating knowledge with crippling banality.

Part 3 – Can We Ever Know?

That of bridled vision
cannot view the cosmic with precision
That seeking what is latent
can construe metaphors but never the patent
That of intra-seasonal duration
cannot envisage the grand evolution
That confined to an infinitesimal neighbourhood
cannot view the galactic brotherhood
That travelling the path to infinity
can never achieve finality

Without Words

Without words   there are no names
without names   there is no delineation
                                  no measure of worth
                                  no discrimination.

Without words   there is no interpretation
without interpretation   there is no fantasy
                                  no gilding the truth
                                  no idols fashioned from imagery.

Without words   there is no dislocation
without dislocation   there is no aberration
                                  no disparity
                                  no alienation.

Without words   there is no deception
without deception   there is no illusion
                                  no betrayal
                                  no confusion.

Without words   there is no coercion
without coercion   there is no manipulation
                       no contrivance
                       no intimidation.

Without words   there is no agitation
without agitation   there is no dread
                       no bearing of arms
                       no lopping of heads.

Without words   there is no action
without action   there is destiny
                       spontaneity
                       integrity.

I for U

At a place of mores   in a moment of time
witnessed by many   accompanied by chime
ordained by ritual   orchestrated to arouse
intent bears witness to an exchange of *vows*.

Yet duration has decreed with wisdom and precision
that *vows* are mere shadows from the glow of affection.
It is the exchange of *vowel* I for U that heralds love and devotion
irrespective of place   indifferent to time   regardless of emotion.

The Deft Touch

Of her many ambrosias

    the deft touch is the most exquisite   with its

        whisper of motion

            perfume of intent

                melody of emotion

                    comfort of presence

                        manner of devotion.

The Relativity of Love and Pain

One who loves cares
One who cares protects
One who protects controls
One who controls coerces

                                          One who coerces controls
                                          One who controls protects
                                                One who protects cares
                                                      One who cares loves

Love is bound
each by the other
What is bound is moderated
each by the all

                                          What is moderated is coerced
                                                      each by the other
                                            What is coerced is pained
                                                        each by the all

Unmediated

To be placid is to rest
To rest is to be composed
To be composed is to be balanced
To be balanced is to be immune
To be immune is to be unmediated
To be unmediated is to be within
To be within is to be content

Wishful Promises

A challenged heart haunts in the depth of night
too petrified to sleep   saturated with fright
What to do for inflamed belief?
Take the following once a day for relief

Promise never again to resurrect old lang syne
never again to convene hindsight
Promise never again to arm with clout
never again to shout

Promise never again to articulate the brain
never again to explain
Promise never again to shame
never again to blame

Promise never again to be enraged
never again to emotionally engage
Promise never again to hate
never again to berate

Promise never again to proffer a choice
never again to have a voice
Promise never again to outpost singularity
never again to dismiss plurality

Thieves All in All

Nature does not favour humanity
in the manner that society favours humanity
but as one for all.

Institutions do not value society
in the manner that humanity favours society
but as one alone.

Brotherhood torches plurality with the match of ideology
searing spontaneity to the ashes of conformity
robbing the many for the few   thieves all in all.

Minority

The minority derives from the majority
the majority are entombed within the minority.
To extinguish minorities is to extinguish the majority
eradicating the totality.

The Counsellor's Lament

If we could inhabit the other and all that is their life
to exist within even a slice of their strife
experience the nature of their determination
we might   at a pinch   proffer counsel of perfection.

But in the provision of tutelage
it is incumbent to acknowledge
that language may be received askew
from that delivered at the pew.

If that is not of sufficient strain
implementation may vary with that ordained
ensuring that the consequences of candour
remain elusive in the hands of another.

Each is without capacity to envisage
the trials of an alternative voyage
the interpretation of communication
the implementation of proposed action.

All that can be imparted
is example long departed.
The tribulations of a single sample
is all we have to gamble.

Dyslexia

This is where dyslexia comes to play
far from literature and its grammatical way
sprawled on white parchment   refreshed by ink
basking in prose   gloriously distinct.

An outlier in the language domain
shamefully estranged   regarded with disdain
eschew the bigotry au communiqué
rejoice in its wisdom and comedic way.

Feel free to wander below
rejoice in their manner say hello
seat yourself amongst the rascality
be infused with their jocularity.

it was sight at first love

        a hard man is good to find

                a heart after my own man

      no taste for accounting

beware of gifts bearing Greeks

          a worse death than fate

                  hoop a cock

         in the time of Nick

(the) grandeur of delusions

                good lickin finger

       madness in my method

a thought for your pennies

       let lying dogs sleep

The Shape of Reality

Life embarks when it must
from an origin unknown
diminishing at a pace unjust.

Disembarking when it must
to a destination unknown
like a flame quickly passed.

Existence marching to anointed progression
returning to nature's Exchequer
according to the contracted transaction.

If what is birth is good
then what is death must also be good
for without the grave there is no neighbourhood.

Be reticent of the dark miasma named fear
it is forever impotent
to that yet to appear.

Your Promised Land

Along your way
in half-score years from now
you will find a jewel
a pearl to endow.

Within the scholar's village
in a dungeon of books
the jewel lies in wait
shining with loving looks.

Head towards the aura of calm
pulsating gently to a heart of true
within distance   golden hair will be in view
finely trickling upon eyes of blue.

With a nature beguiling
and intent of few
lies the most precious gift of all
an I for a U.

With surprise your name will echo
initially from confusion yet devoid of error
sounding the call for a future together
with the promise of love and contentment forever.

Without forethought and with haste
clasp her hand with a gesture grand
remain affixed   do not desist
for she is your promised land.

The Art of Wisdom

The art of wisdom
is to illustrate diversity
on a canvas of clarity
that glimpses beyond the visible
resonates beyond the audible
feels beyond the emotion.

The Imaginary Card

At the dawn of the imaginary year
the imaginary birthday arrives with customary cheer.
'Happy birthday old man' proclaims Self with thoughts in queue
bestowing an imaginary card with words of true.

> *Thank you for your efforts at times of concern and grief*
> *they didn't help much   nor provide relief.*
>
> *Thank you for your views and their expression*
> *they seemed mostly critical   occasioned with suggestion.*
>
> *Thank you for your presence*
> *so often inflammatory to our essence.*
>
> *Thank you for your endeavours at social interaction*
> *forever deciduous   unfit for consumption.*
>
> *Love you xxx*
> *Self*

Be Without

What will you do
   if it is you

        in dwelling   be everywhere
         in thinking   be inclusive
          in giving   be everything
           in listening   be silent
            in participating   be untouched
             in doing   be timely
              in guiding   be innocuous

           be humble without flattery
           be strong without exertion
            be tall without height
           be heard without speaking
           be valued without conceit
         be directional without purpose
        be understanding without judgment

exist without complexity
    achieve without action
        bind without stricture
            shine without light
                proceed without fluctuation
                    receive without entitlement
                        consume without bloating

                            this is what to do
                            now it is you

Virtue Plunges on Affluenzavirus

Virtue has stumbled
on mounting affluence risks.
Nearly seventeen out of the top eighteen virtues
are in the red.

Courage was among the session's better performers.
On the flip side, the hardest hit were equity and justice
after the plug was pulled on a takeover by benevolence
due to the rapid onset of the Affluenzavirus.

In friendship markets, fidelity futures plunged.
Ratings bureau Virtue and Moral (V&M) is calling global despondency
as many implement entitlement measures
to stave off deteriorating material assets.

In their latest report, V&M have sharply downgraded the prospect
of a return to equity in the short term
with initial data from the Non-United Nations
confirming the V&M index at a generational low.

Some have commented that it is difficult to measure
how much virtue will be lost
as a result of the Affluenzavirus.

While the focus
has been on spreading the greedemic
and measuring its growth
recovery will depend crucially
on the prospects for the elusive Affluenza vaccine.

Contentment and Happiness

Contentment is permanent
constant in its contribution   without burden.
Happiness is transient
variable in its contribution   with burden.

To be seduced by the external
is to be without value
To accord with the internal
is to be without poverty.

Perspective

Tomorrow is without promise that much is clear
today   this very moment   is all that is dear
grasp it tightly there is nothing to fear
chime the bell of joy for all to cheer.

Grab your soul by the hand and wander
lie gently beside love and wonder
submerge the moment in gratitude
be mesmerised without attitude.

Take this moment to re-calibrate
dissolve your thoughts   don't postulate
know that there is no grand objective
only a little thing called perspective.

Elders

Only elders can catechise the village
not in the manner of the provedore
but in the wisdom of that before
and that asked by the new age.

The Elegant Solution

The elegant solution knows of no things
no differentiation.

A secondary solution perceives differentiation
without discrimination.

A tertiary solution concedes discrimination
without prejudice.

A quaternary solution endures prejudice
maintaining liberty.

The least solution banishes liberty
losing all.

Vision Impaired

It is with joy to declare
that I am visually impaired

colour blind to black   white   yellow or red
no optics for racial predilection that infuses dread

no sight for gender differentiation
no panorama for religious discrimination

no eye for homophobic reference
no image of behavioural preference

no vision of ethnic dissimilarity
merely an inherent view of singularity

Belief Systems

What (is   )²
What (is not   )²

Knowledge and Belief

knowledge and belief are paired with reluctance
disparate emissaries beleaguered by defiance

one flawless at conception
the other brittle at elucidation

one constant throughout the age
the other variable by sage

one wisdom without dominion
the other power without wisdom

one committed to evidence of absence
the other infused by the absence of evidence

one void of guess
the other conjoined to fear's quest

The Orphan

An orphan is not so due to elders ceased
but one who does not *feel* tethered
to those existing   estranged or deceased.

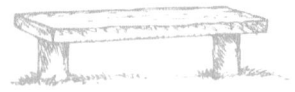

Irrelevant

Coin is irrelevant to wealth
Bluster is irrelevant to worth

Avarice is irrelevant to plentiful
Respect is irrelevant to respectable

Exertion is irrelevant to power
The past is irrelevant to now

Ceremony is irrelevant to grieving
Reward and punishment are irrelevant to teaching

Label is irrelevant to identity
Contrivance is irrelevant to spontaneity

Happiness is irrelevant to contentment
Fear is irrelevant to denouement

Language is irrelevant to veracity
Hope is irrelevant to destiny

The Rake of Hope and Fear

All aboard the locomotive 'Hope'
with its reassuring demeanour and a bright metal cloak
pulling out from station 'Now' in the locale 'Actual'
enroute to destination 'Desire' in region 'Virtual'

Coupled to 'Hope' is the black tender 'Fear'
fuelling delusion with energy and jeer
void the tender   arrest the traction
remain in 'Now'   dismiss the distraction

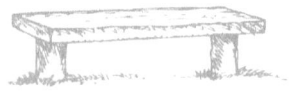

Family

All have parents
Are they family?
Some have in-laws
Are they family?
Some have congregation
Are they family?
Some have obligation
Are they family?

Uncarved love sustained by compassion
Affection faithfully witnessed by parity
Regard for the other as the heritable fashion
Respect consecrated at the altar of individuality
Unconditional inclusion at each resolution
A culture for debate with celebrated rivalry
Recognition of transition without derision
... That is family

Cunabula de Natura

The leaf exists
yet the tree exists onward
the tree exists
yet the earth exists onward
the earth exists
yet the neighbourhood exists onward
the neighbourhood exists
yet the galaxy exists onward
the galaxy exists
yet the universe exists onward
the universe exists
yet the cunabula de natura exists onward

The Cycle of Life

Sleeping prodigiously at beginning   and at end.
Incontinent at beginning   and at end.
Insight at beginning   and at end.
Dependent at beginning   and at end.
Nursed at beginning   and at end.
Wheel-chaired at beginning   and at end.

Reality spherically threads

what was   to what is   to what lies ahead

within the fabric   of space and time

endings are neither ahead   nor behind

all there before   flourishing

each there again thriving.

Place of Last Resort

Dark emotions percolating **dark** thoughts
spoken by **dark** voices thundering **dark** locutions
presented as **dark** arguments arbitrated in a **dark** court
sentenced by **dark** deliberation to a solitary excursion
on a **dark** path to a place of last resort.

No matter how much they loved you
and you them
no matter how much they meant to you
and you to them
it was never enough to procure a future.

Love bleeds from hearts torn open
trickling to anger pooling at despair
all designs and dreams instantly frozen
at a time and space warped by the nadir
of travelling one fewer with eternal rejection.

Names   Perceptions and Destiny

Names delineate
none constant in comprehension
Perceptions illuminate
none equal in interpretation
Destiny adjudicates
none identical in direction

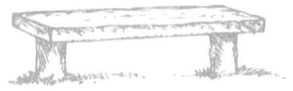

In Perpetuity

For all your nature and your presence
For all your composure and your essence

For all your withins and your withouts
For all your certainties and your doubts

For all your moments in all the places
For all your cards especially the aces

For all your silences and your sounds
For all your steps and your bounds

For all your ups and your downs
For all your smiles and your frowns

For all your laughs and your cheers
For all the birthdays in all the years

For all you are and will be
Love you always in perpetuity

Where Capable Meets Incapable

capable of looking
incapable of seeing through the eyes of others

capable of hearing
incapable of listening through the ears of others

capable of touching
incapable of feeling through the hearts of others

capable of thinking
incapable of interpreting the minds of others

capable of speaking
incapable of communicating to others

capable of delineating
incapable of embracing the unanimity of others

History

History is the shoe-print of the victor
the wealthy and the mighty
rarely the true believer   the poor and the vanquished
never the foot-print of any.

Squandering Longevity

Ignorance vaporises lucidity
blanketing clarity with the fog of irrationality
stoking reaction   escalating entropy
squandering longevity and all its profundity
keep the calendar from the clutch of entitlement
rejoice in the certainty of this very moment.

Undressing Room of Solitude

Peering through circumfused fortification
deflecting the Brownian movement of assignation
ears attuned to the sounds of collision
eyes focused to the refraction of deception.

A remote heart tethered to heightened perception
communicating through the dulcet notes of quietude
resigned to the futility of crafted expression
when not to the appetite of the multitude.

Apprehensive as to the present
knowledgeable as to what must retire
a pantomime of illusion and indifference
amid the despair of a catenary too wide.

Alone   but never lonely
engaged without belonging
forlorn in a sea of company
knowing what   saying nothing.

Turmoil mounting
the proceedings conclude
desperately retreating
to the undressing room of solitude.

In the Now

Life ennobled as a triptych
of the past   the present and the cryptic
a window adorned by a full-length curtain
drawn down at tempo   deemed as certain.

As the schedule encroaches midnight
challenge attains its greatest height
what remains is the now
it is all that has been endowed.

Infancy never rests on aspiration
concerned only with inclination
should it not be that wisdom at ending
advocates that at the beginning?

Hermitage

Solitude is where he lives
where he ponders what he gives
domiciled forward of the bowl
where humanity converses on its bitumen knoll

a hermit in a den
where serenity flourishes devoid of men
within   his favourite things are throughout
they draw a smile when chilling out

a corner reserved for austerity
where words congregate with clarity
at the perimeter lies a shed
a stylographic refuge where restoration is led.

Gummo

I have been in love throughout the years
all of them with you.

I will joke   laugh and despair
all in concert with you.

I will annoy and be incredulous
much to the chagrin of you.

I will interface all that is life
hand in hand with you.

I will focus on that to be done
all through the eyes of you.

I will be warmed and comforted
by the glow that is you.

I will be in love for the years anew
all of them with you.

The Betrayal

In an abode of ritual   on an occasion for cheer
the Queen proclaimed 'Whilst I love you dear   it is your sister
I prefer near
not the youngest she broke my heart
you know   the one sitting two tables apart'

'Sure' said Compassion with a heavy heart
'We will accede to your desire and endeavour to be apart'
'Would you' said the Queen thanking in advance
'I am most grateful that you accede to my preference'

'Like hell she will' cried the table
'we do not agree nor permit her to enable.
An alteration to our table is not for her behest
so dear Queen   please assume your place as our guest'

And with that the first rule of familial love
each child equal   none proclaimed above
was violated   brutally offended
with a daughter's affection forever upended

Edinburgh Castle

All is now misery and battle
at the forlorn Edinburgh Castle
where truth   family and communication
have been debased by ineptness   deceit and confrontation.

The King's enlightenment snuffed by a Dark Age
enabled by the Queen   deployed by Envy   enforced by rage
'I will always do as I trust' cried Compassion with a lashing of dread
and hurt
'but be damned if I engage in the gutter or drown in the dirt'.

Clusters of Affinity

The schisms of disparity broaden chronologically
challenging decency with audacity
gradually coagulating lineage and progeny
into diametric clusters of affinity.

Some stand defiant at the great divide
stoic in their virtue   unrepentant in their stride
firmly obedient to nature's purview
singular in journey   choosing not to choose.

Our Wish

We wish that you like and value who you are
for there is much to admire.

We wish that you continue to place singularity
ahead of bigotry   equity ahead of prejudice
actions ahead of rhetoric   conscience ahead of consensus.

We wish that you continue to be attentive
to the thoughts and aspirations of others.

We wish that you continue to respect and be curious
about the world around you with a glint in your eye
and an awareness of danger.

We wish for you to balance the demands of others
with your own.

We wish that you continue to define wealth
not as that measured by dollars
but the accumulation of experiences adorned with values.

We wish that you continue to be exalted in your views
to be cognisant of but not reliant upon the opinions of others.

We wish that there is no problem so large
no act so terrible   no thought so debilitating
that cannot be shared with us three.

We wish for you to continue to speak with a strong voice
for those unjustly treated   in pain or neglected.

We wish that you will find someone to love
who will love you and commit to you
as much as we know you will to them.

We wish that you continue to keep an open mind
never cease to learn and challenge.

We wish that in your choice of partner
each will love the other more than the previous day
but less than the next.

We wish that you continue to reject second best
and that you pursue your passions with joyous disposition.

While we cannot wish you a life without adversity
we wish that in whatever manner adversity strikes
you continue to stand   strong   proud and true.

We wish that you continue to love the natural world
that you value self   commensurate with that order.

We wish that you have children who will fill your life
with the joy   pride   happiness and love
that you have ours.

The Ageing Season

There are all sorts of food age can't eat
not just fish but varieties of meat
dairy   gluten and sweets are now shite
anything at all once treasured as delight

There are all sorts of hours that age must sleep
not only those nocturnal but the daytime kip
not confined to the sack but any place at all
dismissive of schedule   as the moments befall

There are all sorts of movements that age eschews
those calibrated to speed or subject to review
that requiring split-second precision
or those ending with derision

There are all sorts of thoughts that age thinks
the perniciousness of what the past links
the fatuity of displacing knowledge with ignorance
the fragility of nature's existence

There are all sorts of moments that age compiles
those of love with adoring smiles
events of joy randomly dialled
laughter rolling in the aisle

There are all sorts of concerns that age surrenders
pecuniary status and innuendos
mellowed thought and thinning hair
an appetite for risk and the irresistibility of dare

There are all sorts of matters that age can't abate
the fecundity of time without rebate
the decline of a form progressively jaded
a memory increasingly faded

There are all sorts of tasks that age delights
the pursuit of whimsy that instantly excites
the flagrant disregard for the trite
the presence of thoughts with rare insight

There are all sorts of elixirs that age ingests
those challenging entropy   maintaining zest
promising dexterity of mind and skin
anything at all that defies inflammation

There are all sorts of assets that age can't regain
a body of steel   an efficient brain
yet despite all the pain and the chagrin
One would do it all again with a cheshire grin

Missing You Already

There is resistance that much is credible
infused by repudiation for the inevitable
despite all of life's menus fashioned within and without
it is the meal that has been coveted   of that there is no doubt.

I don't want to leave you at this table
with the shared fruits so abundantly available
not wanting to imagine the briefest moment
of being without you present.

But I do so at the last
embracing in equal part
the poverties and the riches
bestowed to us throughout the ages.

Such is my love for you
that my desire to be with you
will never be extinguished
nor minutely diminished.

The balance-day adjustment has been enacted
the beneficiary recrudescing to the benefactor
willingly with gratitude
reimbursing in magnitude

the profundity of being with you all
throughout the summers   winters   springs and falls
firmly entrenched within the delicacy
that endowed love from each with permanency.

If there was an elixir that secured divinity
it would be declined with certainty
for what would be missed if death was dismissed?
the profundity of reality and youthful bliss.

Bear faithful allegiance to the call for passage
the gates have opened signalling the contracted voyage
love cascades to grief in a torrent of inevitability
let it flow   missing you all already.

Nothing to Fear   Nothing Unjust

Nothing lasts
all is recast

Everything is kindred
each from a shared cupid

In all that is the majesty of reality
lies a balance between beauty and brutality

The prior cannot inhabit the present
the present is unfit for the subsequent

That which is concealed
is inevitably revealed

Nothing is as it is told
the truth lies in what unfolds

Each bound by its nature and capacity
to demand otherwise is to invite anarchy

To not know what is
is to not know what is not

Nothing changes
everything changes

What is and will be is as it must
nothing to fear   nothing unjust

All That Remains

To capture the grail of who you are
to bring into focus what has been afar
transmit your soul through ink with pride
illuminate what lies deep inside.

View the words with grace and gratitude
bear loyal witness to their attitude
yet know these words will be askew
if not faithful to what you do.

Epilogue

The rite de passage has navigated its final contemplation
propelled by the winds of furtive reflection
with only a compass of thought aligning the narrative
and a sextant of knowledge scaling perspective.

Along the journey much was gathered
in moments of need almost none of it mattered
that of rare virtue is all that remained
the presence of love and an epilogue true and plain.

What I now know
what I now understand   is
I will never know
never understand.

The Realist's Interprenary

Action is contrived exertion.
The *after-life* is the transformational continuum of reality.
An *attribute* describes, in part, an event.

The *before-life* is the transformational continuum of reality.
Belief systems are an amalgam of thought, hope and faith.
Birth is the unique agglomeration of fundamental matter.
The *book of life* is authored by reality and annotated by self.

Calamity arises from adherence to that bereft of knowledge.
Construct is imputation of reality.
Contentment is life attuned to reality.
Contingent is dependency on that other than self.

Delineation is the illusion of finitude.
Discourse is the path obliged by the compass of self.
Death is the deglomeration of fundamental matter.
Destiny is the consequence of discourse.
Distress is divergence from self.
Duty is contrived existence.

Eternity is a timeless attribute of reality.
An *event* is the natural outcome of reality.
Existence is the processual nature of reality.

Faith is that exogenous to knowledge.
Fear is uncertainty masquerading as certainty.
Finite is knowledge of an event exceeded by, lessened by or equivalent to another.
Freedom is existence according to self.

Grief is an expression of love for that departed.
Guilt is manipulation servicing nothing other than self-hatred.

Harmony is the fusion of events while maintaining the integrity of each.
Hatred is an inferno sparked from differentiation.
Hope mortgages the certainty of now for the uncertainty of the future.
Hostility arises when the unnecessary is deemed necessary.
Hypocrisy is deviation from self.

Ignorance is the dismissal of what is and retention of what is not.
Impossible is the violation of the laws of reality.
Infinitesimal is no knowledge of an event lessened by or equivalent to another.
Interprenary is a dictionary of interpretations.
Illusions are errors.
Infinity is no knowledge of an event exceeded by or equivalent to another.
Instinct is action devoid of thought.
Insult is provocation, never injury.
Intellect is thought consistent with knowledge.
Introversion is an expression of not belonging.

Kinship is the unity of what was, what is and what will be.
Knowledge is understanding commensurate with reality.

Life is the sum of events procured from the treasury of reality.
Love is an expression of grief for that yet to depart.

Morality is generational adherence to deference.

Natural is an event that occurs in isolation.
Necessary is that sustaining life.
Non-action is existence within one's nature.
Perspective is clarity enhanced by province.
Possible is that consistent with knowledge.
Process is the transformational attribute of reality.
The *purpose of life* is life.

Rationale is the process of thought.
Reality is the interaction of fundamental matter.
Reason is construct embellished as knowledge.

Science is the search for knowledge.
Self is that without thought and exertion.
Simplicity is to exist in harmony with reality.
Singularity is the universal common denominator.
Speculation is the playground of the ignorant.
Spontaneity is the action of self.
Suffering is wanting what cannot be.

Truth is the outcome of knowledge, constant in time and space.

Understanding is an appreciation of knowledge.
Universe is the sum of all events.

Virtue holds steadfastly to self.

Wisdom delineates what is from what is not.

Yours is having without taking.

www.ingramcontent.com/pod-product-compliance
Lightning Source LLC
Chambersburg PA
CBHW020329010526
44107CB00054B/2040